AIR WAR ARCHIV

MESSERSCHMITT Bf 109

THE EARLY YEARS – POLAND, THE FALL OF FRANCE AND THE BATTLE OF BRITAIN

AIR WAR ARCHIVE

MESSERSCHMITT Bf 109

THE EARLY YEARS – POLAND, THE FALL OF FRANCE AND THE BATTLE OF BRITAIN

CHRIS GOSS

FRONTLINE
BOOKS

MESSERSCHMITT Bf 109
The Early Years – Poland, The Fall of France and the Battle of Britain

This edition published in 2017 by Frontline Books,
an imprint of Pen & Sword Books Ltd,
47 Church Street, Barnsley, S. Yorkshire, S70 2AS

ISBN: 978-1-84832-479-4

CIP data records for this title are available from the British Library

For more information on our books, please visit
www.frontline-books.com
email info@frontline-books.com
or write to us at the above address.

Printed and bound by Gutenberg Press Ltd

Typeset in 10/12pt Avenir

CONTENTS

ACKNOWLEDGEMENTS

I would like to thank the following for their assistance in compiling this book: Peter Cornwell, the late Michael Payne, Alfred Price, Bernd Rauchbach, and Gianandrea Bussi.

INTRODUCTION
The Messerschmitt Bf 109

The Messerschmitt Bf 109 single-seat fighter was manufactured in larger numbers than any other warplane of the Second World War. Although the design suffered some drawbacks, limiting its full potential, the Bf 109E – at least for much of the first two years of the war – was generally considered superior to its opponents.

DESIGN AND EARLY PRODUCTION

The requirement for a single-seat fighter was set by the Reichsluftministerium (RLM) in late 1933 and issued to German aircraft manufacturers in 1934. Designed by Professor Willi Messerschmitt and Robert Lusser for the Bayerische Flugzeugwerke AG (later Messerschmitt AG), the Rolls-Royce Kestrel powered Bf 109V1 first flew in September 1935.

The following month it found itself being assessed against its rivals – the Heinkel He 112, Arado Ar 80 and Focke-Wulf Fw 159. Nevertheless, in March 1936 the RLM decided that the Bf 109 would be its choice of fighter, and full production began shortly afterwards.

By then, the Rolls-Royce engine had been replaced by a Junkers Jumo 210 engine. After various prototypes, the initial production version, the Bf 109B-1, the 'Berta', began replacing older fighters such as the He 51 and Ar 64 in the spring of 1937. The B-1 variant was powered by a Jumo 210Da engine (the B-2 with the Jumo 210 Ea) and was armed with a pair of engine-mounted MG 17 machine-guns as well as an MG 17 or MG FF cannon in the propeller shaft. Later B-2s were powered by the Jumo 210G engine. The Bf 109B was to be sent to Spain, as part of the Legion Condor, and therefore would soon be tested in combat.

Messerschmitt continued to develop its new fighter at pace. The Bf 109V8 was still powered by the Jumo 210 Da but now had two guns fitted to the wings. The V8 was then the catalyst for the Bf 109D, the 'Dora', which was powered by the Daimler Benz DB 600Aa. This in turn led to the Bf 109E-1, the 'Emil', which began to appear at the end of 1938.

The E-1 was powered by the DB 601A engine and armed with four MG 17 machine-guns. Arriving on fighter units from spring 1939 onwards, it was the Bf 109E-1 – ably supported by a few Bf 109Ds – that formed both the backbone and teeth of the Luftwaffe's fighter force when war was declared.

DEVELOPMENTS

Pushing onward, Messerschmitt fitted a DB 601Aa and replaced the wing-mounted machine guns with MG FF cannon, resulting in the Bf 109E-3. The subsequent fitment of MG FF/M cannon – which fired improved ammunition – resulted in the Bf 109E-4, which also had improved armour plating and a more angular cockpit.

The fitment of bombs to the Bf 109E began in July 1940 and by the end of the Battle of Britain, one Staffel per Gruppe was Jagdbomber – or Jabo – capable. Such aircraft had the suffixes E-1/B, E-3/B or E-4/B and were fitted with an ETC 500 bomb rack.

Towards the end of the Battle of Britain, a number of Bf 109E-4s were fitted with DB 601N engines and designated E-4/N. A few Bf 109E-7s – the same as the E-4/N but with a centre-line drop tank – and Bf 109E-8s – the same as the E-4 but with a DB 601E engine – also made appearances before the end of 1940.

The Bf 109F, the 'Friedrich', appeared in the skies over the UK from October 1940 onwards. Issued to Stab/JG 51 and I/JG 51, it was the Geschwader Kommodore, Major Werner Mölders, who claimed his 49th, 50th and 51st kills flying a Bf 109F-1 over Kent on the afternoon of 22 October 1940. Fitted with a DB 601N, the Bf 109 F-1 looked different to previous versions in that it had a cantilever tail plane, rounded wing tips, redesigned and symmetrical cowling, and a retractable tail wheel. It was also armed with an engine-mounted MG FF Motorkanone and two MG 17s on the top of the cowling – the F-2 differed only in the calibre of the guns.

Bf 109 WARTIME MARKINGS

Units were normally identified by Staffel, Gruppen or Geschwader badges – such as the red 'R' in a shield for *JG 2 Richthofen* and the black 'S' in a shield for *JG 26 Schlageter*, these names being awarded or granted to the Geschwader – or even the styles of camouflage.

Gruppen were identified by markings – or lack of them – to the aft of the fuselage: cross-nothing for I Gruppe, a horizontal bar for II *Gruppe* and a curved line or vertical bar for III Gruppe. Within each Staffel, aircraft were allocated appropriately coloured numerals in front of the cross – however, Geschwader and Gruppen executives were given a series of chevrons which pointed forward. The principal of these are as follows:

Geschwader Kommodore	Double chevron with vertical or horizontal bar before the cross
Geschwader Adjutant	Single chevron and a vertical bar
Geschwader Technischer Offizier	Single chevron, vertical bar and a hollow disc
Gruppen Kommandeur	Double chevron
Gruppen Adjutant	Single chevron
Gruppe Technischer Offizier	Single chevron and a hollow circle

The colours were as follows:

Geschwader or Gruppen Stab	Blue or green
1, 4, 7 Staffel	White
2, 5, 8 Staffel	Red or black
3, 6, 9 Staffel	Yellow

DRAWBACK IN THE BATTLE OF BRITAIN

The Bf 109E's Achilles heel in the Battle of Britain was its limited operating range of just under 400 miles. To fly over Dorset and Hampshire, for example, Bf 109E units had to forward base either at Cherbourg in northern France or in the Channel Islands. Then, as the phase of battle changed to attacks on London, almost all Jagdgeschwader moved to the Pas de Calais. Even then, London and the Thames Estuary were at the limit of the Emil's range, especially when time for combat – normally 15 to 20 minutes maximum and most flights were of an hour's duration – was factored in.

Most Bf 109s tended to hold off south of London after they had escorted the bombers in to save fuel – and to avoid the British capital's anti-aircraft defences – and met them again on the way out. However, with the RAF soon to go on the offensive and the Jagdgeschwader re-equipping with the Bf 109F, and later the Focke-Wulf Fw 190, this would become less of a problem over northern France and the Low Countries.

GLOSSARY AND ABBREVIATIONS

AA	Anti-aircraft
Adj	Adjutant
Bf	Bayerische Flugzeugwerke (prefix for Messerschmitt Bf 109)
Deckungsrotte	Lookout pair
Deutsches Kreuz in Gold (DKiG)	German Cross in Gold award
Do	Dornier
Ehrenpokal (Pokal)	Goblet of Honour-awarded for outstanding achievements in the air war
Eiserne Kreuz (EK)	Iron Cross (came in First and Second Class)
Ergänzungs (Erg)	Training
Erprobungsgruppe	Experimental Wing
Experte	Ace
Feindflug	Operational flight
Feldwebel (Fw)	Flight Sergeant
Flak	Anti-aircraft
Fluzeugführer (F)	Pilot
Freie Jagd	Free hunting fighter sweep
Führer	Leader
Gefreiter (Gefr)	Leading Aircraftman
Generalfeldmarschall	Air Chief Marshal
Geschwader (Gesch)	Group consisting three Gruppen commanded by a Geschwader Kommodore (Gesch Komm)
Gruppe (Gr)	Wing consisting three Staffeln; commanded by a Gruppen Kommandeur (Gr Kdr. Gruppe number denoted by Roman numerals (e.g II).
Hauptmann (Hptm)	Flight Lieutenant/Captain
He	Heinkel
Holzauge	Lookout
Ia	Operations Officer
Jabo	Fighter-bomber
Jagd	Fighter

Jagdgeschwader (JG)	Fighter Group
Jagdgruppe (JGr)	Fighter Wing
Ju	Junkers
Kampfgeschwader (KG)	Bomber Group
Kette	Three aircraft tactical formation similar to RAF vic
Lehrgeschwader (LG)	Technical Development Flying Group
Leutnant (Lt)	Pilot Officer/2nd Lt
Luftflotte	Air Fleet
Major (Maj)	Squadron Leader/Major
Me	Messerschmitt (used by RAF)
Nachrichtenoffizier (NO)	Communications Officer
Oberfeldwebel (Ofw)	Warrant Officer
Obergefreiter (Ogefr)	Senior Aircraftman/Cpl
Oberleutnant (Oblt)	Flying Officer/1st Lt
Oberst	Group Captain/Colonel
Oberstleutnant (Obstlt)	Wing Commander/Lt Col
Reichsmarschall	Marshal of the Air Force
Ritterkreuz (RK)	Knight's Cross
Ritterkreuz mit Eichenlaub (EL)	Knight's Cross with Oakleaves
Rotte	Two aircraft tactical formation; two Rotten made a Schwarm; commanded by a Rottenführer
Rottenflieger	Wingman
Schlacht (S)	Ground attack
Schwarm	Four aircraft tactical formation commanded by a Schwarm Führer
Seenotflugkommando	Air Sea Rescue Detachment
Sonderstaffel	Special Staffel
Stab	Staff or HQ; formation in which Gr Kdr and Gesch Komm flew.
Stabsfeldwebel (Stfw)	Senior Warrant Officer
Staffel (St)	Squadron (12 aircraft); commanded by a Staffel Kapitän (St Kap). Staffel number denoted by Arabic numerals (eg.2)
Technischer Offizier (TO)	Technical Officer
Unteroffizier (Uffz)	Sergeant
Werk Nummer (Wk. Nr.)	Serial Number
Zerstörer (Z)	Destroyer/Heavy fighter
Zerstörergeschwader (ZG)	Heavy Fighter Group

A Bf 109D of II (S)/JG 134 which became II/JG 142 in November 1938. This unit would then become II/ZG 142 in January 1939, and, in May 1939, would become II/ZG 26 Horst Wessel. It would not convert from the Bf 109D to the Bf 110 until early 1940. For much of its early life, this unit was based at Werl, near Dortmund, where this photograph was taken.

Bf 109B/Ds of II/JG 142 outside a hangar at Werl. Also in the photograph is a Junkers Ju 34 (centre) and what appears to be a Heinkel He 100 (left).

In May 1939, II/ZG 141 became I/ZG 76 and between June and August 1939, converted to the Bf 110. This photograph shows Bf 109D-1s Red 6+- and Red 9+- of 5/ZG 141. The badge under the cockpit is the coat of arms of Olmütz where the unit was based from May until August 1939 – a blue and white chequered bird on a red background.

Many Bf 109Bs soldiered on during the war at training schools. This Bf 109B-1, Wk Nr 1032 and coded TC+KB, first flew on 18 August 1937 with the civilian code D-ISJE. It is thought it was used in the development of the Bf 109F wing, but this photograph was taken in 1940 at an unknown training school.

TC+KB ended its days on 5 April 1943 when it was badly damaged in an accident at Prenzlau and subsequently written off. At the time it was on the strength of Überprüfungsschule (für) Erweiterter Luftwaffen-Führerschein, the examination school for the Luftwaffe advanced flying certificate.

These Bf 109Ds are from ZG 141 and taken at Pardubitz, during the winter of 1938–39. The unit appears to be 2./ZG 141 due to the numeral colours and lack of markings behind the fuselage cross.

Bf 109Bs (identifiable by the absence of wing-mounted guns) having just rolled off the production line, presumably at Augsburg. Apart from national identifiers, they appear to have no other markings.

A Bf 109B of Jagdschule 1 at Werneuchen during 1939. Note the camera under the port wing root.

A Bf 109E is used as the backdrop for a funeral, believed to be that of *Obergefreiter* Kreidt of 3/JG 53, at Wiesbaden-Erbenheim. Kreidt was killed on 13 June 1939.

ABOVE: The Bf 109 was tried and tested in the Spanish Civil War. Here, seventeen Bf 109 E-1s of Jagdgruppe 88 (J/88) are parked up – they had arrived in Spain in early 1939. The sign to the right reads 1 Staffel, which was commanded by *Hauptmann* Siebelt Reents.

OPPOSITE: At the start of the war, *Oberleutnant* Lothar Ehrlich was serving in I/JG 52. He is seen here on a Bf 109B/D when he was with I/JG 433 (named I/JG 52 from May 1939). In March 1940, he moved to the recently formed III/JG 52 to command 8/JG 52. He scored the Gruppe's first kill of the French campaign, a Curtiss Hawk south of Metz, on 18 May 1940. Having arrived on the Channel coast on 22 July 1940, on 24 July he, together with *Major* Wolf-Heinrich von Houwald (*Gruppen Kommandeur*), *Oberleutnant* Herbert Fermer (*Staffel Kapitän* 7/JG 52) and *Gefreiter* Erich Frank (7/JG 52), was shot down and killed over the Channel by Spitfires of 54 Squadron. Ehrlich's place was taken by *Oberleutnant* Günther Rall, who would become a highly successful fighter pilot with a distinguished post-war career. The following day, Fermer's replacement, *Oberleutnant* Wilhelm Keidel, and then his replacement, *Oberleutnant* Willy Bielefeld, were both shot down and killed over the Channel together with *Leutnant* Hans Schmidt, the *Gruppen Adjutant*. After such losses, III/JG 52 was withdrawn from the Channel Front on 1 August 1940, being redeployed to Zerbst for rest and refit.

Nine Bf 109E-1s of J/88. The first three on the right carry the gun-toting Mickey Mouse emblem of 3 *Staffel*. At the time, 3 Staffel was commanded by *Oberleutnant* Hubertus von Bonin, who had taken over from *Oberleutnant* Werner Mölders. Mölders, for his part, had taken over from *Oberleutnant* Adolf Galland.

Harmonising the guns of a Bf 109D, in this case an aircraft of J/88 coded 6•84.

This Bf 109B, coded 6•32, has tipped over onto its nose suffering minimal damage, possibly at La Cenia. The tail shows at least ten kill markings. The only pilots to achieve this were *Leutnant* Peter Bodden (ten), *Hauptmann* Harro Harder (eleven), *Hauptmann* Werner Mölders (fourteen), and *Hauptmann* Wolfgang Schellmann (twelve).

ABOVE: Bf 109B/Ds of J/88 getting airborne from La Cenia during the Spanish Civil War.

BELOW: The Bf 109B of 4/JG 132 flown by *Leutnant* Jürgen Moller. Moller later transferred to fly Bf 110s with 5/ZG 1 and was captured on 2 June 1940, when he collided with an RAF fighter over Dunkirk.

Leutnant Jochen Schypek of 3/JG 76 photographed with his mechanic in front of his Bf 109E-3, Wk Nr 1266, Yellow 13.

Leutnant Franz Fiby of 3/JG 2 in a Bf 109E-3 coded Yellow 13. Note the Richthofen badge; the aircraft would have the blue 3/JG 2 pennant on the cowling. Fiby survived the war.

Groundcrew working on a Bf 109D-1 of Stab/JGr 152 at Biblis, Germany, in September 1939. Formed from I/ZG 52, the unit existed, under the command of *Hauptmann* Wilhelm Lessmann, from 24 September 1939 to 6 January 1940. After this it re-equipped with the Bf 110, and later that year became II/ZG 2. The aircraft carries the *Gruppen Kommandeur*'s chevron on the fuselage.

Another view of the *Gruppen Kommandeur*'s Bf 109D-1. During its short period of existence, the unit was based at Biblis, then Odendorf and, finally, Düsseldorf Lohausen. The officer who has just received the Iron Cross Second Class is *Leutnant* Hartmann Grasser of 3/JGr 152. He transferred to fly Bf 109s with Stab/JG 51 in October 1940 and survived the war, having shot down 103 aircraft and been awarded the Ritterkreuz mit Eichenlaub.

This view of a busy Luftwaffe airfield, with numerous types present, is believed to be Lachen Speyerdorf in the autumn of 1939. The Bf 109D-1 coded White 3, seen here in the foreground, carries the Bernburger Jäger badge under the cockpit and Black Hand emblem on the cowling, which identifies the unit involved as *Oberleutnant* Waldemar von Roon's 1/ZG 2. The darker camouflaged aircraft carries the chevron of *Gruppen Kommandeur Hauptmann* Hannes Gentzen. For the period between 21 September 1939 and 30 January 1940, I/ZG 2 was known as JGre 102. Gentzen was killed in an accident whilst flying a Bf 110 of I/ZG 2 on 26 May 1940, by which time he had shot down eighteen aircraft. Von Roon died of wounds two days after being shot down on 6 November 1939.

Bf 109s of 1/JG 53 at Wiesbaden-Erbenheim in 1939. At this time, 1/JG 53
was commanded by the soon-to-be famous *Oberleutnant* Werner Mölders.

A Bf 109E-1 of 3/JG 76, probably the aircraft flown by *Staffel Kapitän Oberleutnant* Franz Eckerle, at Stubendorf in August 1939. Amongst the four pilots sitting nearest the aircraft is *Leutnant* Jochen Schypek (became a prisoner of war on 25 October 1940) on the far left, whilst *Leutnant* Hans Jürgen Westphal is believed to be third from the left.

I/JG 76 prepares for war at Stubendorf during August 1939.

With the Wk Nr 6009, this Bf 109E-1, White 9, is a /JG 76 aircraft photographed at Stubendorf during 1939. Just visible is the Bf 109E of the *Gruppen Kommandeur*, *Hauptmann* Wilfried von Müller-Rienzburg.

A Bf 109E-3 showing the markings of a *Gruppen Kommandeur* of III Gruppe. No unit markings are evident on what appears to be a brand new fighter.

Bf 109s photographed at Strausberg, east of Berlin, at the start of the war. The markings on the nearest Bf 109E denote a III Gruppe aircraft. The only known units to be based at Strausberg were I/JG 20 and 10/JG 2.

Coded Yellow 2, this aircraft of 3/JGr 152, and which is believed to be a Bf 109D-1, is pictured having its guns harmonised at Biblis, late 1939. At the time 3 Staffel was commanded by *Oberleutnant* Emil Schnoor who had a very varied combat career. Awarded the Deutsches Kreuz in Gold, he would survive the war having shot down twenty-three aircraft – the first of which was a Morane 406 on 24 September 1939.

Opposite: This highly decorated officer, who has just been awarded the Eiserne Kreuz II, is *Oberleutnant* Wilhelm Balthasar, the *Staffel Kapitän* of 1/JG 1. He received the honour, which accompanied those he gained in Spain with J/88, on 23 September 1939. He stands in front of White 1 which also carries the *Staffel Kapitän*'s pennant on the radio mast. Balthasar would be awarded the Ritterkreuz mit Eichenlaub and, with his score standing at forty-seven, was shot down and killed on 3 July 1941 when commanding JG 2.

A Bf 109E1 of 1/JG 53 – that coded White 10. On 30 September 1939, this aircraft suffered engine failure and crash-landed at Kirchberg-Hunsrück. Despite looking relatively intact, the back of the aircraft was broken and it was written off. The pilot was uninjured.

This Bf 109, coded CA+NK, had the Wk Nr 1361. It was one of a batch of mostly E-3s with a few E-4s built by Erla late in 1939 and into 1940. After it was selected for modification to an E-4/B, it became the V26 prototype, and participated in various extended range fighter-bomber tests associated with the new E-7. It is believed that it was written-off following a crash sometime in August 1940. Here it is loaded with a 250kg bomb. The G.SCH on the panel by the spinner is believed to be an abbreviation for Glykol-Schutzöl.

This Bf 109E-3 of 3/JG 76, Wk Nr 1251 and coded Yellow 11, was shot down by French fighters from *Groupe de Chasse* I/3 (GC I/3) during the Phoney War – more specifically just before lunchtime on 22 November 1939. Its pilot, *Leutnant* Heinz Schulz, crash-landed at Rémeling-les-Puttelange and was captured unhurt. His fighter was later displayed in Paris.

Another Phoney War victim of *Groupe de Chasse* I/3, again on 22 November 1939, was the 1/JG 76 Bf 109E-3 seen here. With the Wk Nr 1304 and coded White 1, it was flown by *Feldwebel* Karl Hier.

After his encounter with *Groupe de Chasse* I/3 on 22 November 1939, *Feldwebel* Hier put his aircraft down almost intact at Goersdorf in north-eastern France. The aircraft was captured by the French, repaired and then flown for evaluation purposes.

Like his aircraft, Hier was also captured on 22 November 1939 – though would be subsequently released after the fall of France in 1940. He flew during the Battle of Britain with 4/JG 54 (formerly 1/JG 76). He managed to shoot down a total of fifteen aircraft before he was reported missing in action on 15 November 1940.

Before being posted to 1/JG 53 in January 1940, *Unteroffizier* Heinrich Höhnisch flew with Stab/JG 53. This photograph shows him climbing into a Bf 109E-1 at Wiesbaden-Erbenheim in November or December 1939. The significance of the Cat emblem and the colours of the 12 on the fuselage (presumed to be green) cannot be confirmed. Höhnisch would have a successful career with 1/JG 53 before being shot down and taken prisoner on 9 September 1940, by which time he had accounted for a total of six French and British aircraft.

A Bf 109E-1 coded Red 7 of 2/JG 20. This photograph was probably taken at Brandenburg-Briest between September and November 1939. At the time 2 Staffel was commanded by *Oberleutnant* Albrecht 'Minni' Freiherr von Minnigerode; the unit was re-designated 8/JG 51 in July 1940. Note the Black Cat emblem of 2/JG 20 on the cowling.

The Boot emblem on the nose of this Bf 109E-1 identifies it as an aircraft from I/JG 77. Commanded by *Hauptmann* Johannes Janke, this unit did not move west until July 1940, and did not take part in the Battle of Britain until being subordinated to JG 51 at the end of August 1940, when it was based at Marquise. This photograph is believed to have been taken at Odendorf late 1939 or early 1940.

Oberleutnant Rudolf Unger, *Gruppen Adjutant* of JG 53 pictured in a in a Bf 109E-1 at Wiesbaden-Erbenheim, October 1939. Note that despite being a Stab aircraft, this fighter carries numerals on the fuselage. Note also the oversized wing cross. Unger would move to Stab/JG 54 in 1940, taking command of 2/JG 54 in June 1940. He shot down his first aircraft on 4 September 1940 and was posted away to be an instructor in June 1941. It is believed he survived the war.

Three pilots from 3/JG 2 gathered in front of a Bf 109E-3. The picture was probably taken at Frankfurt Rebstock in the winter of 1939–1940. Left to right are unidentified, *Oberfeldwebel* Franz Jaenisch and *Leutnant* Franz Fiby. The tip of the spinner is painted yellow for 3 Staffel, and just visible on the cowling is the 3/JG 2 badge – a blue pennant with a yellow sword and the word 'Horrido!'.

Feldwebel Fritz Kahlmeier in the cockpit of Yellow 8+I, a 9/JG 53 Bf 109 (9/JG 53 was commanded by *Oberleutnant* Ernst Boenigk). Note the just visible *Pik As* (Ace of Spades) badge on the cowling. Kahlmeier would be killed in a take-off accident at Hoppstäden on 11 May 1940 and posthumously promoted to *Leutnant*.

A close up of *Feldwebel* Fritz Kahlmeier of 9/JG 53 in the cockpit of what is thought to be a Bf 109E-1 coded yellow 8+I.

A photograph of groundcrew and armourers at work on Red 10 of 2/JG 20. This unit's *Staffel Kapitän*, *Oberleutnant* Albrecht 'Minni' Freiherr von Minnigerode, would be shot down over Holland and taken prisoner on 11 May 1940.

A Bf 109E of 1/JG 76, coded White 1, pictured at Wien-Aspern in the autumn of 1939. This aircraft, which had the Wk Nr 6009, was usually flown by *Leutnant* Anton Stangl.

Opposite: Hauptmann Walter Kienzle took command of 5 (Jagd) Trägergruppe 186 at Jever at the end of February 1940. It was intended that II/186 (T) would operate from the German aircraft carrier *Graf Zeppelin* but in the meantime carried out normal fighter duties. An experienced pilot, Kienzle, who had previously been *Staffel Kapitän* of 2/JGr 101, was posted to JFS Magdeburg at the end of May 1940, after which his Staffel became 3/Erprobungsgruppe 210, commanded by *Oberleutnant* Otto Hintze. In September 1940, Kienzle was posted to Stab/JG 26 but was shot down and taken prisoner on 30 September 1940.

Oberleutnant Karl Lommel, the *Staffel Kapitän* of 1/JG 52, looks on as a kitten plays on the cowling of a Bf 109E-1 at Lachen-Speyerdorf in early 1940. The Running Boar emblem of I/JG 52 was red and blue, with a black boar. Lommel took command of 1 Staffel in March 1940 and was not posted away until he was given temporary command of I/JG 52 in November 1941 following the wounding of *Oberleutnant* Karl-Heinz Leesmann. By this time Lommel had shot down three aircraft. In mid-1942 was posted away to be a fighter pilot instructor. It is believed he survived the war.

Bf 109s of 9/JG 53 at Wiesbaden-Erbenheim in early 1940. Visible are Yellow 6+I and, nearest to the camera, Yellow 7+I.

A group of NCO pilots of I/JG 53 in early 1940. Those individuals who have been identified are *Unteroffizier* Heinrich Höhnisch (second from left; became a prisoner of war on 9 September 1940), *Unteroffizier* Josef Wurmheller (centre; 102 victories, awarded Ritterkreuz mit Eichenlaub, killed in action 22 June 1944), and *Unteroffizier* Herbert Tzschoppe (second from right; captured on 15 September 1940).

Oberleutnant Günther Domaschk, *Technischer Offizier* of II/JG 2, photographed in early 1940. He was posted away in 1941 to a series of training appointments and survived the war.

Engine runs on an early Bf 109E-3. It is possible that this
aircraft belonged to *Major* Dr Erich Mix of III/JG 2, a unit
which was formed at Magdeburg-Ost in March 1940.

Bf 109s of 9/JG 53 at Wiesbaden-Erbenheim, early 1940. Note that two of the Bf 109s have darkened camouflage to the rear of the fuselage and tails. The pilot in the centre is believed to be *Leutnant* Josef Volk.

Unteroffizier Kurt Sauer of 9/JG 53 poses for the camera in early 1940 on what is believed to be a Bf 109E-3. Note the distinctive camouflage and the size of the *Pik As* emblem. Sauer would survive the Battle of Britain, though he was reported missing near the Molodechno area of Belarus just after shooting down his fifth enemy aircraft on the evening of 27 June 1941. At the time he was flying a Bf 109F-2, which, with the Wk Nr 6689, was coded Yellow 4+I.

Just visible below the cockpit of this Bf 109D is the Bernburger Jäger emblem that denotes that its unit is JGr 102. Furthermore, the 8, black or red, indicates 2 Staffel.

A Bf 109E-4, Yellow 3+-, of 6/JG 27. This photograph is said to have been taken at Bönninghardt where II/JG 27 was based from 3 to 9 May 1940 – but the camouflage indicates that it might have been taken later than this.

On 19 May 1940, *Oberleutnant* Lothar Krutein of 4/JG 2 was shot down near Tournai, probably during combat with Hurricanes of 85 Squadron. He managed to crash-land and was taken prisoner, but was released when France capitulated. The crash site of his White 5+- was discovered by members of his Staffel. Krutein's subsequent career is not known, apart from that he was *Staffel Kapitän* of 4 (Erg)/SKG 10 in 1943, responsible for training Jabo pilots on the Focke-Wulf Fw 190.

What appears to be a Bf 109E-1, Yellow 3+-, of 6/JG 27 having come to grief in northern France. The damage appears superficial. It was recorded that this incident took place on 21 May 1940, but this cannot be substantiated. *Leutnant* Herbert Schmidt was lost in a Bf 109E-1, Wk Nr 3859 and coded Yellow 3+-, on 30 September 1940; Schmidt bailed out badly wounded and his fighter crashed into a wood near Haslemere in Surrey.

Bf 109Es of 1/LG 2 seen at Montecouvez-Nord, France, between 23 May and 4 June 1940. White 2 was normally flown by *Unteroffizier* Fridolin Volkmer. The aircraft of 1/LG 2 carried a black disc with a white cross behind the fuselage cross; 2/LG 2 carried a top hat badge, whilst 3/LG 2 fighters were adorned with Mickey Mouse holding an umbrella.

Bf 109Es of III/JG 26 believed to have been photographed at Villacoublay. The whole Geschwader, less I/JG 26, arrived at Villacoublay on 17 June 1940, III/JG 26 leaving five days later. Note the small numerals on Black 4 and Black 2. The only record of a Black 4 was Bf 109E-4 Wk Nr 3735 which crashlanded on the Isle of Grain on 23 September 1940. The pilot, *Feldwebel* Arnold Küpper, was captured. By then, this aircraft had the standard yellow cowling and Schlageter shield. It also carried the 8 Staffel Adamson badge of an old man running and brandishing a walking stick.

The Adamson staffel badge on the aircraft flown by *Leutnant* Hans Joachim Geburtig. Geburtig would be shot down near Samer on 21 June 1941 whilst at the controls of Bf 109F-2 Wk Nr 5521. When he had recovered from his wounds, he was given command of 10/JG 26 on 18 July 1942 – only for his Focke-Wulf Fw 190 to be shot down by anti-aircraft fire off Littlehampton on 30 July 1942; he was captured.

Hauptmann Karl Ebbighausen, the *Staffel Kapitän* of 4/JG 26, in his colourful Bf 109E. Ebbighausen had flown with J/88 in Spain, hence the Mickey Mouse emblem, shooting down three aircraft. He was wounded in action on the evening of 19 May 1940 during combat with Hawker Hurricanes of 615 (County of Surrey) Squadron and managed to crash-land his Bf 109E-3, which was coded White 8+-. *Hauptmann* Herwig Knüppel was shot down and killed in the same action. Ebbighausen then took command of II/JG 26 as the *Gruppen Kommandeur*, but was reported missing in action over the Channel on 16 August 1940. He had shot down seven aircraft by this stage of the war.

Bf 109Es of 6/JG 27 photographed at either Evère or St Trond in Belgium during May or June 1940. The aircraft sport varying camouflage schemes, but at least two have the arms of the City of Berlin on the cowling.

Leutnant Julius Neumann of 6/JG 27 in a Bf 109E coded Yellow 3+-. Neumann would shoot down one aircraft in the Battle of France – a Fokker TV south of Rotterdam on 10 May 1940. He also claimed a victory in the Battle of Britain, in this case a Spitfire off the Isle of Wight on 16 August 1940. Neumann was shot down flying a Bf 109E-4, Wk Nr 1455 and coded Yellow 6+-, on 18 August 1940. He crash-landed on the Isle of Wight and was captured.

Bf 109s of 1/JG 53 at Charleville, France, in June 1940. The nearest fighter, White 6, has two kill markings on its tail – this aircraft was normally flown by *Oberfeldwebel* Alfred Müller, who scored his second kill on 26 May 1940. Müller was shot down and taken prisoner on 15 September 1940, his total kills remaining at two.

Two views of the wreckage of a Bf 109E-1, White 13 of 1/JG 3, which crash-landed at Grandvillers, France, having suffered engine failure. It is believed that this incident took place on 4 July 1940.

Close examination of this picture reveals that the main section of wreckage on the right is a Daimler-Benz DB 601 engine. At 10.52 hours on 6 July 1940, *Unteroffizier* Hermann Marquardt of 1/JG 3 crashed on take-off from Grandvilliers in a Bf 109E-1, Wk Nr 4051. He and *Obergefreiter* Otto Freudenberg were killed in the resulting crash, the latter became a victim when the fighter crashed into tented accommodation on the edge of the airstrip.

The graves of *Obergefreiter* Otto Freudenberg and *Unteroffizier* Hermann Marquardt following the crash on 6 July 1940.

An unusual view along the fuselage of *Leutnant* Josef Volk's Yellow 2+I of 9/JG 53 – an image taken in the early summer of 1940. Volk claimed a Potez 63 and a LeO 451 on 31 May 1940, but achieved no kills in the Battle of Britain. He was shot down by a Hurricane of 605 (County of Warwick) Squadron on 11 November 1940. Taken prisoner, he had been flying a brand new Bf 109E-8, Wk Nr 4888 and coded yellow 12+I.

Leutnant Josef Volk's Bf 109 showing the two kills he achieved on 31 May 1940. Volk flew with 9/JG 53.

A Bf 109E-7, coded White 12, of 1/LG 2 clearly showing the 1 Staffel badge. The date and location of this mishap are not known.

Bf 109Es of 9/JG 26 photographed in protective sandbag pens and underneath camouflage netting at Caffiers in the Pas de Calais in early summer 1940.

Loading fifty-kilogram bombs to a Bf 109E-4/B during 1940.

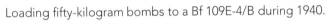

An air-to-air shot of a group of unidentified 1 Staffel Bf 109s, coded white 1, 4 and 10, on patrol in the summer of 1940.

A *Schwarm* of Bf 109s of 6/JG 27 led by *Oberleutnant* Julius Neumann. Note the camouflage demarcation and the positioning of the tail swastika. Yellow 10+- was normally flown by *Unteroffizier* Fritz Gromotka, who would survive the war with twenty-nine victories, having been awarded the Ritterkreuz. The other two aircraft would be Yellow 2+-, normally flown by *Unteroffizier* Heinz Uebe, who would be wounded in action on 8 August 1940 having shot down two aircraft, and Yellow 4+-. The latter was flown by *Feldwebel* Erich Krenzke, who would be taken prisoner of war on 31 May 1942 with his victory score standing at eleven.

Feldwebel Walter Meudtner of 3/JG 51 in the cramped cockpit of his Bf 109E-1/E-3 in the early summer of 1940.

A pair of Bf 109Es of I/JG 3 at Grandvillers, France, in July 1940. The machine to the left, an E-4, has a chevron on the fuselage showing it to be a Stab I/JG 3 aircraft. The marking following this could be a circle, which would indicate this aircraft to be flown by the Gruppe's *Technischer Offizier.*

Groundcrew at work on a Bf 109E-4 of Stab I/JG 3 on the airfield at Grandvillers, again in July 1940. The tail appears to have two kill markings on it. The only Stab I pilot who had two kills by the start of the Battle of Britain was *Oberleutnant* Walter Fiel, who was posted to command 8/JG 53 on 8 September 1940. Fiel was shot down and taken prisoner on 2 October 1940.

Executive officers of I/JG 3 at the Gefechtstand (command post) at Grandvillers, July 1940. The identity of the two officers is not known.

Another view of Bf 109Es of I/JG 3 beneath camouflage netting at Grandvillers, July 1940. The aircraft to the left, an E-4, has a chevron on the fuselage showing it to be a Stab I/JG 3 aircraft.

The battle-axe identifies the unit of this Bf 109 as being III/JG 3, the picture probably being taken at Desvres, France. It is believed that this is a Gruppenstab aircraft and, if so, the numeral, believed to be 3, would be green. The spinner is black and white, cowling and upper surfaces yellow to canopy and heavily mottled fuselage.

A line-up of Bf 109E-4s of an unidentified unit. The cowlings on these aircraft were yellow and they appear to be carrying letters as opposed to numerals on the fuselage.

A Bf 109E-4 of 3/JG 2 being flown by *Leutnant* Franz Fiby. Clearly visible are the 3 Staffel emblem on the cowling, the Richthofen badge and angular yellow 14. Note that there is no demarcation line between the upper fuselage and lower fuselage camouflage.

An unidentified pilot from what is believed to be JG 2, probably celebrating his return after a successful mission. He is wearing the bulky 10-76B kapok filled life preserver and what appears to be a pair of first pattern *Nitsche und Günther Splitterschutzbrille* (anti-splinter) glasses.

Bf 109Es of 3/Erprobungsgruppe 210 at Denain in the summer 1940. During the Battle of Britain, 3 Staffel lost just three aircraft in combat. The last of these was its *Staffel Kapitän, Oberleutnant* Otto Hintze, in Bf 109E-4/B Wk Nr 2024, Yellow, 6 on 29 October 1940. Hintze would be captured, albeit wounded. He was awarded the Ritterkreuz in absentia.

There are at least six kill bars visible on the forward part of the tail of this Bf 109E-4 of III/JG 3, Wk Nr 1559 and coded White 1+, which was pictured at Desvres in France in the autumn of 1940. This aircraft was flown by *Hauptmann* Wilhelm Balthasar who by the end of the Battle of Britain had thirty-six kills to his name. Balthasar brought this aircraft with him from 1/JG 1, retaining the White 1 but adding the III Gruppe vertical bar after the fuselage cross.

Leutnant Horst Marx in front of his Bf 109E-1/B at Denain, Belgium, in July or August 1940. Marx would be shot down and taken prisoner on 15 August 1940 whilst flying a Bf 109E-4/B coded Yellow 3.

This busy scene of an open air workshop for the Bf 109Es of III/JG 26 was taken at Caffiers during July or August 1940.

Oberleutnant Gerhard Schöpfel, the *Staffel Kapitän* of 9/JG 26, in his Bf 109E-4. Note the manufacturer's plate below the badge. Schöpfel would take command of III/JG 26 on 22 August 1940 when *Major* Adolf Galland took command of JG 26. He remained with JG 26, having become *Kommodore* in December 1941, until January 1943. A series of short staff appointments followed before he returned to operational flying in May 1944. He was awarded the Ritterkreuz in September 1940 and survived the war with forty-five kills to his name.

A mixture of Bf 109Es of I and II/JG 77, probably photographed at Aalborg in August 1940. The nearest aircraft shows it to be that of the *Gruppen Adjutant, Leutnant* Herbert Kunze, and, if so, is probably an E-4 with the Wk Nr 5102. Kunze was shot down and killed on 15 September 1940 when his Bf 109E-4, this time with the Wk Nr 3759 but carrying the same fuselage markings, crashed at Lympne, in Kent. I./JG 77 moved to Marquise-West in the Pas de Calais on 25 August 1940 and became subordinate to JG 51. It was re-designated IV./JG 51 in November 1940.

Bf 109Es of 6/JG 27 photographed at either St Trond, Belgium, in May 1940 or Crépon, France, in August 1940. Note the II Gruppe Bear badge on the cowlings of both fighters.

The scene at Caffiers, France, in August 1940 as groundcrew
construct blast pens for the Bf 109Es of III/JG 26.

Opposite: As a sentry walks past, groundcrew are pictured working on a Bf 109E-1 of 1/JG 53 at Cherbourg-Ost, August 1940. The true reason for the red band, which replaced the *Pik As* badge, is thought to have been either an official order to hide the identity of the Geschwader or a personal grudge between senior officers. However, for much of the Battle of Britain, JG 53 carried this red band and only at the end of 1940 was it removed and the *Pik As* badge reapplied.

A further picture taken at Caffiers during August 1940. The Yellow 1 together with the pennant on the aerial would indicate this aircraft belonged to *Oberleutnant* Gerhard Schöpfel, *Staffel Kapitän* of 9/JG 26, or his replacement, *Oberleutnant* Heinz Ebeling. Note the Schlageter badge on the righthand Bf 109E and the Höllenhund emblem of 9/JG 26 on Yellow 1.

Opposite: Unteroffizier Heinrich Höhnisch of 1/JG 53, on the left, pictured with his mechanic at Cherbourg-Ost, August 1940. Note the red ring on the cowling and inertia starter handle.

This photograph shows *Feldwebel* Heinrich Höhnisch of 1/JG 53 on his Bf 109 at Rennes in July 1940 – the red band has not yet been applied.

A stunning photograph of Bf 109Es of 5/JG 53 taxying out at Cherbourg-Ost, August 1940. The *Staffel Kapitän* at this time was *Oberleutnant* Rudolf Goy. Of interest is the fact that 5 Staffel adopted grey fuselage markings and all of its aircraft appear to have yellow cowlings, whilst some have the red band. Note the nearest Bf 109E-3 has two kill markings on the tail; at the end of August 1940, only *Unteroffizier* Willi Holdermann and *Leutnant* Eduard Berwanger of 5/JG 53 had two kills – both were killed in action on 26 August 1940.

One of the junior pilots on 1/JG 53 was *Unteroffizier* Werner Karl who flew a Bf 109E-1, Wk Nr 3584 and coded White 14. This photograph was taken in early August 1940 before the *Pik As* badge was replaced by the red band. Werner Karl was shot down in this aircraft, crash landing near Hythe, on 2 September 1940 – by which time the red band had been applied and noted by RAF intelligence officers.

A Bf 109E of 3/JG 51 seen at Pihen/St Inglevert, in the Pas de Calais, during August or September 1940. The officer is believed to be *Oberleutnant* Richard Leppla, the Staffel Kapitän of 3/JG 51. He was awarded the Ritterkreuz and survived the war.

A Bf 109E-4 of III./JG 53. Note the red band around the cowling and the vertical bar denoting III Gruppe at the rear of the fuselage. The spinner appears to be red as well, which should denote 8 Staffel, though there is evidence that this Staffel used black tactical markings. It is not known if this photo was taken at Brest-Süd or Villaize/Guernsey, the Gruppe moving to Le Touquet on 24 August 1940.

An early loss for JG 2. At 07.10 hours on 13 August 1940, *Oberleutnant* Paul Temme, Gruppen Adjutant of I/JG 2, force-landed his Bf 109E-3, Wk Nr 5068, in a field near the airport at Shoreham-by-Sea in West Sussex and was captured none the worse for wear. His fighter carried the Richthofen badge below the cockpit and the chevron was in black. At the top of both sides of the rudder there were three kill markings, these referring to a Potez 63 south of Sedan on 15 May 1940 and two Spitfires south-west of Calais on 26 May 1940.

The day before Temme's crash-landing, *Oberleutnant* Albrecht Dress, Gruppe *Technischer Offizier* of III/JG 54, crash-landed his Bf 109E-4, coded white <-+, at Hengrove near Margate. During the same combat Dress claimed his first and last kill of the war. Formerly known as I/JG 21, III/JG 54 was operating from Guines in the Pas de Calais at the time. The emblem was based on the Jesau cross; I/JG 54 had been formed at Jesau the previous summer.

Thought by some to be the Bf 109E-4 flown by an *Unteroffizier* or *Oberfeldwebel* Keller, this is in fact Black 6 of 2/JG 3, which suffered an accident returning from combat on the afternoon of 15 August 1940. The pilot at the time was *Feldwebel* Hans Ehlers. Ehlers had been shot down before on 18 May 1940, having just experienced his first victory. He would end the Battle of Britain with four kills. He was later awarded the Ritterkreuz, but was killed in action on 27 December 1944 with his score of victories in the region of fifty-five.

Opposite: Hauptmann Hans-Karl Mayer, *Staffel Kapitän* of 1/JG 53, sitting on the tail of his Bf 109E-4 coded White 8 at Cherbourg, 13 August 1940. The damage to the fuselage was inflicted by an RAF fighter the previous day when he shot down his tenth and eleventh victims. His seventh kill, as indicated on the rudder, occurred on 14 May 1940 – it is assumed that official confirmation had not yet been received. Mayer would be awarded the Ritterkreuz but was reported killed in action, as *Gruppen Kommandeur* of I/JG 53, on 17 October 1940.

A Bf 109E-4 of 2/JG 3, that with the Wk Nr 1990 and coded Black 13, pictured lying in a field near Maidstone, having been shot down, on 18 August 1940. The pilot, *Oberleutnant* Helmut Tiedmann, was the *Staffel Kapitän* of 2/JG 3. He was brought down whilst on a bomber escort sortie over Kent in the early afternoon of 18 August, his fighter was hit in the glycol system, which forced him to shut down the engine. He managed to crash-land near Leeds Castle in Kent and was on the run for nearly twelve hours before being captured. Note the red Taztelwurm badge on the cowling.

Another view of *Oberleutnant* Tiedmann's Bf 109E-4. Tiedmann had shot down his first aircraft on the evening of 16 May 1940. On 30 May 1940, he was given command of 2/JG 3 by which time he had a total of four kills; his last of the Battle of France, on 16 June 1940, would be his sixth. He would score the first kill of I/JG 3 in the Battle of Britain, a Hurricane on 15 August.

Seen by the tail of his Bf 109E-3 coded Black 1 is *Hauptmann* Horst Tietzen of 5/JG 51. Tietzen's first kill after the Battle of France, his third overall, was a Blenheim on 27 June 1940. By the time this photo was taken he had shot down eighteen, the most recent being a Hurricane near Canterbury in the afternoon of 16 August 1940. He would get his twentieth just before his death in combat on 18 August 1940, his body being washed ashore later near Calais. He had shot down seven aircraft in Spain and would be posthumously awarded the Ritterkreuz two days after his death.

Opposite: Hauptmann Rolf Pingel arrived to command I/JG 26 at Audembert on 22 August 1940. Having shot down ten aircraft with 2/JG 53, his first kill as *Gruppen Kommandeur* was a Spitfire on 29 August 1940 (the first of two that day). By the end of the Battle of Britain, he had shot down sixteen aircraft and was awarded the Ritterkreuz on 14 September.

The rudder of the Bf 109E-4, Yellow 1, flown by *Oberleutnant* Gerhard Schöpfel, the *Staffel Kapitän* of 9/JG 26. On 18 August 1940, his unit bounced the Hurricanes of 501 Squadron, claiming four kills. *Leutnant* Gustav Sprick of 8/JG 26 also claimed one, whilst *Leutnant* Josef Bürschgens of 7/JG 26 claimed a further two. The six lost by 501 Squadron in this combat were Pilot Officer John Bland, who was killed, Pilot Officer Ken Lee, Pilot Officer Franciszek Kozlowski and Sergeant Don McKay, who were all wounded, whilst Flying Officer Robert Dafforn and Flight Sergeant Percy Morfill both baled out unwounded. It is believed that Schöpfel shot down the first four pilots.

Hauptmann Rolf Pingel in the cockpit of his Bf 109. Just visible are the flags of the countries over which he had flown by November 1940, these being those of, from left to right, Great Britain, France, Belgium, Poland and Spain.

Major Adolf Galland in his Bf 109E-4 of JG 26. The nose appears yellow and the aircraft carries the Schlageter shield, his personal Mickey Mouse emblem and the *Kommodore*'s chevron.

This photo of Galland's Bf 109E-4 shows it carrying a 300-litre tank. His Bf 109E-4 at this time was Wk Nr 5819.

Major Adolf Galland in his Bf 109E-4. Later, he had a
telescopic gun sight fitted to his Bf 109E-4/N Wk Nr 5819.

A photograph of *Feldwebel* Herbert Bischoff's Bf 109E-1, White 9 of 1/JG 52, after being shot down near Margate on 24 August 1940. The crash-landing predates the painting of cowlings yellow by days. Note the heavy mottled camouflage and white and black spinner.

Unteroffizier Wilhelm Kaiser of *Hauptmann* Dr Albrecht Och's 9/JG 3 survived the crash-landing of his Bf 109E-1, coded Yellow 12+I, at Camber in East Sussex on 24 August 1940. The aircraft was noted to have a yellow rudder and wing tips. Kaiser had only arrived on 9/JG 3 at Desvres three days before and this was thought to have been his first operational flight.

With its fuselage covered in oil, this is the wreckage of Bf 109E-4 Wk Nr 5587, coded Yellow 10, of 6/JG 51 after it was shot down on 24 August 1940. Aircraft of II/JG 51 carried a Weeping Bird emblem aft of the fuselage cross instead of the more expected horizontal bar.

The pilot of 5587, *Oberfeldwebel* Fritz Beeck, was credited with his fourth kill of the war just before he was shot down and crash-landed at East Langdon in Kent. On the tail were three kill bars with the dates 7 July, 29 July and 15 August 1940, which prove that this was Beeck's personal aircraft – he was credited with a Spitfire east of Dungeness at 21.40 hours on 7 July 1940, another Spitfire north of Dover on 29 July 1940 and finally a Hurricane on 15 August 1940.

New pilots tended to fly the higher numeral aircraft. This is Bf 109E-1 White 15 of 1/JG 53 which was flown by *Gefreiter* Josef Bröker. He had arrived on 1/JG 53 mid-August 1940 and he was shot down on 25 August 1940 in this aircraft. Note that the red band has been applied to the cowling. Bröker crash-landed intact at Buckland Ripers in Dorset, only to be burnt setting fire to his fighter.

The rudder of *Hauptmann* Hans-Karl Mayer's Bf 109E-4, White 8 of 1/JG 53. His thirteenth kill was a Hurricane near Salisbury at 18.45 hours on 15 August 1940, the victim possibly being Flying Officer Gordon Cleaver of 601 (County of London) Squadron. This would suggest that the photograph was being taken between 16 and 24 August 1940, when Mayer shot down his fourteenth aircraft.

Same rudder, same pilot, but this time with seventeen kills depicted. Mayer (with forage cap) shot down two Spitfires on 26 August 1940, one of which was flown by Sergeant Cyril Babbage of 602 (City of Glasgow) Squadron.

This photograph was taken at Étaples in mid-September 1940, by which time Mayer had been given command of I/JG 53. The kill markings (twenty-nine in total) have been modified slightly – he was credited with twenty-two kills (the last being on 15 September 1940) by the time of his death in action on 17 October 1940. The eight that appear to have lines through them could refer to barrage balloons. It is interesting to note that at this stage he still flew White 8 as opposed to one with the *Gruppen Kommandeur's* chevron.

Siegfried Schnell standing in front of the rudder of his Bf 109. The nine kills indicated would date this photograph as having being taken between 2 September (his 6th kill) and 11 September 1940 (his 11th). The only other dates for his kills are 7 and 8 September 1940, but what order they are in his tally cannot be confirmed. Schnell's Bf 109 is believed to be an E-3 Wk Nr 1232. Schnell would be awarded the Ritterkreuz mit Eichenlaub, but was killed in action on 25 February 1944 having shot down ninety-three aircraft.

Another up and coming ace was *Leutnant* Julius Meimberg of 4/JG 2, seen here at Mardyck, France, in September 1940. On 6 September 1940, he shot down two Spitfires, his fifth and sixth kills, near Ashford. His next kill was not until 10 October 1940; he would end that year with nine kills. Meimberg would be awarded the Ritterkreuz and survive the war with fifty-three kills – albeit having been shot down and wounded a number of times.

Personnel from the highly successful Stab III/JG 51 seen at St Omer/Clairmarais in the summer of 1940. They are, left to right, *Oberleutnant* Otto Kath (Adjutant), *Leutnant* Werner Pichon-Kalau (*Technischer Offizier*), *Leutnant* Herbert Wehnelt (*Nachrichten Offizier*), and *Hauptmann* Hannes Trautloft (*Gruppen Kommandeur*). Trautloft would take command of JG 54 on 24 August 1940 and end the Battle of Britain with eight kills. Kath (who moved with Trautloft to JG 54) would shoot down two, as would Wehnelt. Pichon-Kalu would also accompany Trautloft to JG 54, shooting down six by the end of the Battle of Britain. All four survived the war.

Hauptmann Helmut Wick of I/JG 2 in the cockpit of his Bf 109E-4. Note he is wearing the Ritterkreuz which was awarded on 27 August 1940. He would be awarded the Eichenlaub on 6 October 1940.

Oberleutnant Anton Stangl of 5/JG 54 in the cockpit of a Bf 109E-1/E-3. Stangl's favourite aircraft number was Black 14. Indeed, he was flying Bf 109E-4 coded Black 14, Wk Nr 1277, when he collided with another aircraft over Kent on 1 September 1940. He baled out and was captured with his kill total standing at six.

Whilst this photograph appears to feature an identical Bf 109E-1 to the one of *Feldwebel* Herbert Bischoff's White 9 of 1/JG 52, which was lost on 24 August 1940, it is in fact *Feldwebel* Heinz Uerling's Bf 109E-4, Wk Nr 1261. Coded White 12 of 1/JG 52, this fighter was shot down at Westbere, Kent, on 2 September 1940. Note that the cowling has not been painted yellow.

On 4 September 1940, *Hauptmann* Wolfgang Lippert arrived from 3/JG 53 to take command of II/JG 27, then based at Fiennes. The lion shows the aircraft to be from Stab II/JG 27. The bear emblem of II Gruppe is just visible on top of the pennant, whilst the *Gruppen Kommandeur's* chevron can also be seen. The aircraft has the yellow cowling which was adopted by all Bf 109 units at the end of August 1940. Lippert received the Ritterkreuz in September 1941 and was then shot down and taken prisoner, badly wounded, on 23 November 1941 with his total of kills standing at twenty-five (with another five from Spain). He died of his wounds, whilst still in hospital, on 3 December 1941.

Another successful former JG 53 pilot was *Hauptmann* Hans von Hahn, one time *Staffel Kapitän* of 8/JG 53, who took command of I/JG 3 at Colombert on 27 August 1940. His first victory with his new unit would be on 5 September 1940 (his eighth) and he would add another three to that before the Battle of Britain was over. His Bf 109E-4 carried a stylised chevron on the fuselage in that all three sides were solid. In addition to the Hahn badge, on the yellow nose, it carried a green Tatzelwurm. Von Hahn would be another Ritterkreuz winner and would survive the war with thirty-four kills.

The wreckage of Bf 109E-4 Wk Nr 1506, coded White 5+I, of 7/JG 53. *Unteroffizier* Hans-Georg Schulte crash-landed this aircraft just short of RAF Manston in Kent late on the afternoon 6 September 1940. Schulte was credited with seven kills, the last being claimed during his last mission.

Schulte's Bf 109E-4 being readied for public display. This aircraft had a white spinner, cowling and rudder and apparently a red band had been over-painted on the cowling. Note also the swastika has been over-painted.

Two pilots of 5/JG27 pictured on their airfield at Montreuil during the early part of the Battle of Britain. The individual on the right is *Oberleutnant* Erwin Daig. On 9 September 1940, Daig, at the controls of a Bf 109E-1, was shot down in combat over West Sussex. That afternoon Daig was part of the escort for a large formation of bombers whose target was London docks. On the approach his 109 was hit and began to lose speed. After the bombers had delivered their deadly cargos upon London, Daig found himself intercepted by two British fighters and his already-damaged aircraft was struck again. He dived away from his pursers and tried to reach a bank of broken cloud which was at a height of about 9,000 feet. 'Before I reached the safety of this cloud,' he later recalled, 'one of my attackers caught up with me and again opened fire. Once again I felt the shock of more hits, at which point I put my 'plane into yet another dive. This time I kept going until I was almost at ground level, when I headed straight for France, trying to escape by flying at low level.' Daig never made it home. The British fighters pursued him relentlessly and his Messerschmitt took more hits. 'By now my 'plane had started to smoke and I was having trouble seeing. I threw back my cockpit hood to see if this would help, but all that happened was that the engine just died. I then saw a gently rising slope, similar to a meadow, that was profusely covered with old lorries. I quickly lost speed and then the 'plane hit the ground. The chase was finally over!' The Bf 109 came to ground on a small private landing strip used by the residents of nearby Parham House before the war (it is today the home of Southdown Gliding Club). The lorries Daig referred to, along with abandoned cars and farming implements, had been scattered across the field as anti-glider and anti-invasion measures. Daig also recounted his first hours as a prisoner of war: 'I was well treated … an English officer asked me if I had any firearms, to which I replied "no". I was then taken from the crash site to a nearby army base where I was shown to the commanding officer who offered me a glass of whiskey.'

119

During and after the Battle of Britain some ninety or so captured Bf 109s took part, in one form or another, in various fund raising efforts. Here *Oberleutnant* Erwin Daig's Messerschmitt Bf 109E-1, Wk. Nr 3488, is on display during the War Weapons Week in Nuneaton, Warwickshire.

A Bf 109E-7 in a salvage depot in the UK during the Battle of Britain. The Mickey Mouse emblem identifies the unit as 3/LG 2. This is the Bf 109E-7 flown by *Unteroffizier* August Klick who crash-landed on the Isle of Sheppey on the afternoon of 15 September 1940 after being shot down by a pilot of 19 Squadron.

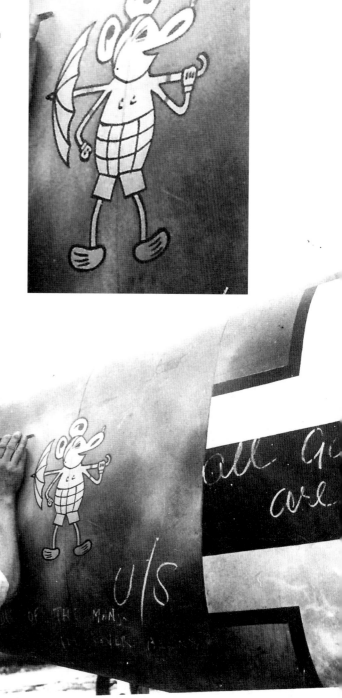

Another view of *Unteroffizier* August Klick's Bf 109, complete with its Mickey Mouse emblem, in the RAF salvage yard. Note that 3/LG 2 used red/brown numerals instead of yellow. The spinner, cowling and upper surfaces up to the canopy and rudder were yellow and the remaining camouflage described as 'cloudy grey on fuselage, wings battleship grey and light blue underneath.

About to go on display in Trafalgar Square is this Bf 109E-1, Wk Nr 6147 and coded Black 5, of 2/JG 27. Just after midday on 15 September 1940, *Unteroffizier* Andreas Wallburger crash-landed near Uckfield in Sussex due to combat damage. The RAF investigators noted that this aircraft was fitted with a bomb rack, that the factory codes BZ+NG were still just about visible, the spinner was coloured red and white, cowling yellow and the Black 5 was edged with red. At the time 2/JG27 was commanded by *Oberleutnant* Gerd Framm and based at Guines.

Feldwebel Walter Meudtner of 3./JG 51. Meudtner flew throughout the Battle of Britain but was unable to claim any victories. On 26 September 1940, Meudtner was flying with his *Staffel Kapitän*, *Oberleutnant* Richard Leppla, when they bounced two Hurricanes over the Channel. The RAF fighters are believed to have been flown by Flight Lieutenant G.R. Edge and Pilot Officer W.M.C. Samolinski of 253 Squadron. Both Hurricanes were shot down; Edge was wounded and Samollinski killed. Meudtner, flying Bf 109E-4 Wk Nr 5369, also failed to return. As there were no witnesses for the destruction of the Hurricanes, they were not claimed.

Feldwebel Walter Meudtner of 3/JG 51 photographed just before he was killed in action on 26 September 1940. Just visible below the cockpit is the mountain goat badge of I/JG 51 – a black goat on top of a black mountain peak, on a white diamond in a blue shield.

Just visible on the yellow cowling of this Bf 109E is an eagle's head and wing which stretches almost the entire length of the cowling. This denotes that the unit is 6/JG 52, which was based at Peuplingues from 25 September to 5 October 1940. For much of this time the unit was commanded by *Oberleutnant* Rudolf Resch, who joined from 3/JG 77 on 6 October 1940. Resch was be another Ritterkreuz winner, but would be killed in action commanding IV/JG 51 on 11 July 1943 – by which time he had claimed to have shot down ninety-four aircraft.

Pushing a Bf 109E-4 of 2/JG 52 into its blast pen at Coquelles, September 1940. Other photographs show this have the Wk Nr 1268, be coded Black 5, and have eight kill bars on the tail. This aircraft was flown by *Oberleutnant* Helmut Bennemann who shot down his eighth aircraft on 15 September 1940. Bennemann would be awarded the Ritterkreuz and survive the war having shot down ninety-three aircraft.

In September 1940, 9/JG 26 became the III/JG 26 Jabo Staffel and would be commanded by *Oberleutnant* Heinz Ebeling – who is believed to be in the cockpit of this Bf 109E-1/B. Ebeling would collide with Rottenflieger Feldwebel Walter Braun on 5 November 1940, with both being captured. Ebeling's last kill before he became a fighter-bomber pilot was his eighteenth on 18 September 1940. He was awarded the Ritterkreuz whilst a prisoner of war.

One of 2/JG 53's Bf 109E-3s, Black 14, being pushed back into a blast pen at Le Touquet during September 1940. It would appear that this particular aircraft was generally flown by *Oberfeldwebel* Franz Kaiser who had shot down five aircraft by the end of the Battle of Britain. He would be shot down and taken prisoner over the Mediterranean on 21 April 1942.

The twenty-seven bars pointing upwards, starting 11 May 1940, and fourteen downwards on this Bf 109E-4, Wk Nr 1559 and coded White 1, show the air and ground successes of its pilot, *Hauptmann* Wilhlem Balthasar. Balthasar commanded 1/JG 1 in the Battle of France before being posted to be a fighter instructor at Werneuchen. He was then recalled to command III/JG 3 at the start of September 1940. His kill on 4 September 1940 (his twenty-fourth of the war) would see him also being wounded and he did not score again until 23 September. His twenty-seventh kill would be a Spitfire at 14.25 hours on 27 September.

Hauptmann Wilhlem Balthasar preparing for a mission. His Bf 109E-4 carried the III/JG 3 axe on the yellow cowling whilst it also carried I/JG 1's Jesau cross (carried also on III/JG 27 aircraft) below the cockpit.

An official press photo of *Hauptmann* Wilhlem Balthasar alongside the rudder of his Bf 109E-4.

Black 4 of 2/JG 53 parked up at Le Touquet during September or October 1940. For much of the Battle of Britain, 2/JG 53 was commanded by *Oberleutnant* Ignaz Prestele who took over from *Hauptmann* Rolf Pingel when he was posted to command I/JG 26 on 21 August 1940. Prestele was killed in action on 4 May 1942, whilst Pingel would be captured 10 July 1941.

Oberleutnant Ignaz Prestele, Staffel Kapitän of 2/JG 53, in his Bf 109E-4 at Le Touquet in September or October 1940. Note that the red band on the cowling appears to have been overpainted.

A mixture of Bf 109Es of I/JG 3 photographed at Wizernes. The nearest two aircraft, Yellow 9 and Yellow 2, are from *Oberleutnant* Eberhard Bock's 3 Staffel. Black 3 is from *Oberleutnant* Helmut Meckel's 2 Staffel. I/JG 3 was based at Wizernes from 20 September 1940 to 16 February 1941. Note that the Tatzelwurm badges are painted around on the yellow cowlings.

Working on the Bf 109E-4 which, coded White 7, was the personal aircraft of *Oberleutnant* Hans Ohly of 1/JG 53. It would appear that I/JG 53 liked flying aircraft with the same numbers more than most and when Ohly became *Staffel Kapitän* on 1 September 1940, he retained the same numeral as opposed to White 1. He would continue flying White 7 after 1/JG 53 converted to the Bf 109F. The rudder shows four kills, the most recent a Hurricane on 25 August 1940. Just visible is the red band around the cowling.

A close-up of a 250kg bomb underneath a Bf 109E-4/B
of 3/JG 53 at Le Touquet during October 1940.

Groundcrew working on what appears to be a Bf 109E-1 of 3/JG 53 at Le Touquet, October 1940. Note that the spinner now has an aerodynamic faring over the central hole.

An inertia starter handle inserted in a Bf 109E-3/B of 3/JG 53 at Le Touquet, October 1940. Note the armoured windscreen and patching around the MG FF barrel, both of which would indicate field modifications.

Starting a Bf 109E-3 of 3/JG 53, Le Touquet, October 1940.

A brand new Bf 109E with the markings of the *Gruppen Kommandeur* of I/JG 53, the red band visible on the nose. This photograph was taken at Le Touquet in October 1940 so is either the aircraft of *Hauptmann* Hans-Karl Mayer (who was killed in action on 17 October 1940 flying a Bf 109E-7, Wk Nr 4138) or *Hauptmann* Hans-Heinrich Brustellin (who replaced him, former *Gruppen Kommandeur* of I/JG 51).

The remains of a Bf 109E-4 on the beach at Cap Gris Nez pictured after it had started being broken up. Other photographs seem to indicate this was an aircraft from I/LG 2, which was based at Calais-Marck during the Battle of Britain. This unit lost Bf 109E-4s in this general area on 24 August 1940, 23 September 1940 and 12 October 1940, but positive identification of this particular casualty has not been possible.

A Bf 109E-3 of 3/JG 77. With the Wk Nr 5104 and coded Red 13, *Gefreiter* Karl Raisinger crash-landed this E-3 at Harvey's Cross Farm near North Saltdean, East Sussex, during the early afternoon of 25 October 1940. The cowling and rudder were yellow. On the port side of the cowling was written 'Rocho' in red. The port side also had a line of flags below the canopy, one of which was Danish, whilst just above the Wk Nr were three victory tabs. Raisinger arrived with his unit at Marquise on 28 August 1940, flying his first mission three days later. He first flew Red 13 on a test flight on 8 October 1940. He flew it operationally on ten occassions before being shot down on his 25th operational flight. Raisinger claimed just one kill, a Hurricane on 17 October 1940. He later stated that Red 13 belonged to another officer who was off sick, which would explain the kill markings anomaly.

Overleaf: Gefreiter Karl Raisinger's Bf 109E-3 on public display, doing its bit for the war effort.

Another loss on 25 October 1940 was this Bf 109E-4, Wk Nr 1988 and coded Black 7, of 5/JG 54. *Oberleutnant* Jochen Schypek flew this aircraft regularly after it replaced that with the Wk Nr 2759, which had been lost on 28 August 1940 whilst being flown by *Unteroffizier* Karl Kleemann. Schypek first flew 1988 on 28 September 1940. When he was shot down Schypek had been on his 196th operational flight of the war. Black 7 had four kill markings on the tail which accorded with his kills on 14 May 1940 (a Curtiss Hawk), 27 June 1940 (Bristol Blenheim), 9 September 1940 (Spitfire) and 5 October 1940 (another Spitfire). His aircraft was reported to have a yellow cowling and tip of rudder, spinner green and white with a red tip. The aircraft was originally coded 3 and the JG 54 Lion of Aspern badge was in the process of being painted.

Oberleutnant Hans 'Assi' Hahn, *Staffel Kapitän* of 4/JG 2, was posted to command III/JG 2 at the end of October 1940 having been awarded the Ritterkreuz (which he is wearing) on 24 September 1940. His last kill with 4/JG 2 was a Spitfire on 15 October 1940 (his twentieth). The rudder belongs to the Bf 109E-4 of *Oberfeldwebel* Siegfried Schnell who is to Hahn's right. Schnell shot down his thirteenth and fourteenth kills on 30 September 1940 – which would date this photo as being taken at Beaumont-le Roger between 1 and 20 October 1940. Just visible to the right is *Gefreiter* Rudi Miese of 4/JG 2 who would be shot down and captured, badly wounded, on 15 November 1940 whilst flying Bf 109E-4 Wk Nr 5947, White 10. Schnell would be awarded the Ritterkreuz mit Eichenlaub but was killed in action 25 February 1944, having shot down ninety-three aircraft.

The Bf 109 'White 13' of 7/JG54, Wk Nr 3576, which, flown by Unteroffizier Arno Zimmermann, was shot down on 27 October 1940. Zimmermann crash-landed near the water tower in Lydd. Note the positioning of the numeral and lack of Gruppe marking after the fuselage cross.

THE MESSERSCHMITT Bf 109 THE BATTLE OF BRITAIN

The forty-two kills on the rudder of this Bf 109E-4, I *Gruppen Kommandeur*'s chevron and the 3/JG 2 Horridoh pennant all prove that this aircraft was flown by *Hauptmann* Helmut Wick. This photograph was taken after 15 October 1940, but before his 43rd kill on 29 October – by which time Wick had been promoted to Major and given command of JG 2. He was reported missing in action off the Isle of Wight, whilst flying Bf 109E-4 Wk Nr 5344 coded <-+, just under one month later. Wick claimed fifty-six air combat victories and been awarded the Ritterkreuz mit Eichenlaub.

Major Helmut Wick of JG 2 in his Bf 109E-4 showing the 3 Staffel Horridoh badge and Richthofen shield. It cannot be said for certain if this photograph was taken when he was *Gruppen Kommandeur* I/JG 2 or Geschwader Kommodore.

Artistic licence on the ETC500 bomb rack fitted to a Bf 109E-4/B of 3/JG 53, October 1940.

This photograph was taken by an Italian pilot at a Belgian airfield at the end of the Battle of Britain. Clearly a Bf 109E-4/B, the unit is possibly 3/Erprobungsgruppe 210 and taken at Denain. By this stage of the war, one Staffel per Bf 109 Gruppe was a Jabo staffel. (*via Bussi*)

I/JG 1, which became III/JG 27, carried numerals on the nose and no markings fore and aft of the fuselage cross. During the Battle of Britain, the highest numeral recorded on a loss was Black 15 on a Bf 109E-4, Wk Nr 2790, flown by *Oberleutnant* Günther Deicke, *Staffel Kapitän* of 8/JG 27. Deicke was shot down and taken prisoner on 15 October 1940. All the nearest aircraft appear to have yellow cowlings. Markings like this appear to have been discontinued when III/JG 27 converted to the Bf 109F in 1941. It is also possible that these Bf 109Es are serving with Ergänzungsgruppe/JG 27, which was formed in November 1940 at Oldenburg. The earliest known Executive Officer of this unit was Hauptmann Erich Gerlitz, who was posted to be *Staffel Kapitän* of 2/JG 27 in April 1941.

The black triangle on this Bf 10E-4/B identifies it as a Jabo from II(Schlacht)/LG 2. Previously a Henschel Hs 123 ground attack unit, it flew fighter-bomber missions from Calais-Marck from September 1940 onwards. This particular aircraft, Wk Nr 5593 and coded White N, was flown by *Oberfeldwebel* Josef Harmeling of *Oberleutnant* Heinrich Vogler's 4/LG 2. It was shot down over North Weald on 29 October 1940. This is an early photograph of it going on display as in later photographs the Mickey Mouse emblem has been cut away for a trophy. Note the yellow cowling and rudder and bullet strikes on the fuselage.

A Bf 109E-1/B carrying two fifty-kilogram practice bombs.

A Bf 109E-3, coded White 9, of an unidentified unit. The rudder and underneath of the engine appears to be white and the spinner aperture covered over.

This Bf 109, either a E-4/N or E-7 variant, is fitted with a 300-litre centre-line tank. The aircraft appears to be very new, and still retains the factory codes.

Leutnant Oskar Ziesig on the wing of a Bf 109E of 8/JG 2. The aircraft's full code would be Black 5; III/JG 2 used the wavy line after the fuselage cross to denote III Gruppe. Ziesig was posted away to be a night fighter pilot but after being wounded he returned to day fighters with 3/JG 1 and 6/JG 51. He survived the war.

A Bf 109E-4 of 1/JG 2, Wk Nr 5159 and coded White 9, which was formerly the aircraft of *Geschwader Kommodore Oberstleutnant* Harry von Bülow-Bothkamp who was posted away on 2 September 1940.

On 1 November 1940, *Oberleutnant* Hermann Reifferscheidt was shot down in 5159/White 9, near Chichester and taken prisoner. He had arrived on 1/JG 2 at the start of September 1940, claiming one kill (a Hurricane of 145 Squadron off the Isle of Wight on 27 October 1940) before he himself was shot down by a Hurricane of 145 Squadron. Immediately before his demise, he claimed to have shot down a Hurricane of 213 Squadron, the only RAF loss in that area that day.

Stabsfeldwebel Franz Willinger in front of a Bf 109E-4 of 8/JG 2. For much of the Battle of Britain, 8 Staffel was commanded by *Oberleutnant* Bruno Stolle. It was based at Le Havre Octeville until 28 August 1940, then Oye-Plage until 14 September 1940, before returning to Octeville until 20 October. Apart from a few days in the south of France, the remainder of 1940 would be spent at Bernay.

161

Leutnant Leopold Wenger getting into the cockpit of his Bf 109B/D at Jagdfliegerschule 5 (JFS 5), Wien-Schwechat, in October or November 1940. The badge on the nose appears to be a hand, similar to the badge of 1/JGr 102. The recognised badge of JFS 5 was a blue, white and yellow shield, incorporating a Bf 109. Wenger would be posted to JG 2 and become a successful Jabo pilot, being awarded the Deutsches Kreuz in Gold and Ritterkreuz. With the fighting in Europe drawing to a close, Wenger was killed in action on 10 April 1945.

A Bf 109B of JFS 5 being started by means of an inertia starter at Wien-Schwechat. Note the camera underneath the wing.

An air-to-air shot of a Bf 109B of JFS 5 over the Austrian countryside during October or November 1940. Though not apparent in this image, the number 9 lies within a yellow fuselage band.

With the Wk Nr 420, ND+EZ was a Bf 109D. Its last unit was Luftdienst Kommando 1/11 – its service history is unknown.

In October 1940, III/JG 52, which had been badly mauled in July 1940 and withdrawn to Zerbst for rest and refit, moved to Bucharest-Pipera ready for operations in the Balkans. The Gruppe was then commanded by *Major* Gotthard Handrick and this Bf 109E-4, coded White 3, is from 7 Staffel, which was commanded by *Hauptmann* Erwin Bacsilla. This aircraft still retains the yellow spinner and cowling evident on Bf 109s operating over the UK from the end of August 1940. This picture shows Handrick giving King Michael I of Romania a guided tour of a Bf 109.

This air-to-air shot is from a series of photographs taken by Italian pilots. The unit operating this Bf 109E-4/B has defied identification. (*via Bussi*)

A second picture from the series taken by Italian pilots. It is known that the unit in question was based on the Franco-Belgian border during November 1940. (*via Bussi*)

Our last image from the series taken by Italian pilots. The white tip of the 250-kilogram bomb shows it to be an inert practice bomb. (*via Bussi*)

Werner Mölders in the cockpit of a Bf 109E-4 at Pihen in the summer of 1940.

Opposite: The fifty-five kills on the rudder of this Bf 109 show it to be that of *Major* Werner Mölders of JG 51. By the end of the Battle of Britain, Mölders had shot down fifty-four aircraft; his fifty-fifth was a Hurricane near Ashford on the afternoon of 1 December 1940. He and his wingman, *Oberleutnant* Hartmann Grasser, bounced Flight Lieutenant Alec Ingle and Flying Officer Cyril Passy of 605 (County of Warwick) Squadron, shooting down and wounding both – Ingle's Hurricane crashed at Harrietsham and Passy's at Hollingbourne in Kent. Mölders was not flying a Bf 109E but a Bf 109F-1, Wk Nr 5628 and with the factory code SG+GW. His first flight in the Bf 109F-1 was 9 October 1940 and during the Battle of Britain he shot down five RAF fighters flying this variant. He handed over his Bf 109E-4, Wk Nr 3737 and coded <-+-, to *Hauptmann* Hans Asmus. This was the aircraft Asmus was flying when he was shot down and captured on 25 October 1940. The forty-nine kill markings on the rudder initially led the RAF to think they had captured Mölders, not Asmus.

Three members of 8/JG 2 pictured in late 1940. They are *Stabsfeldwebel* Franz Willinger, *Leutnant* Oskar Ziesig and *Feldwebel* Karl Ebert. By the end of 1940, Willinger had shot down seven aircraft, Ziesig none and Ebert at least two. Willinger would later fly with JG 51 and be commissioned, only to be killed in an accident whilst serving with Erprobungsstelle Rechlin on 5 February 1943. Ebert continued flying with 8/JG 2 until 1944, being awarded the Ehrenpokal and Deutsches Kreuz in Gold. He would be commissioned, then fly with 10/JG 2 only to be wounded on 16 March 1944. He returned to command 11/JG 2 and is believed to have survived the war with at least eighteen kills.

Possibly photographed at Abbeville-Drucat in the winter of 1940, this is *Oberleutnant* Walter Horten, *Geschwader Technischer Offizier* of JG 26, in front of *Hauptmann* Gerd Schöpfel's Bf 109E-7 of Stab III/ JG 26. Horten flew alongside *Major* Adolf Galland throughout the Battle of Britain, shooting down five aircraft. He was taken off operational flying because of his aeronautical engineering skills and, with his brother Reimar, would later develop the revolutionary Horten flying wing.

A Bf 109E-7 of 2/JG 3 photographed at Wizernes during the winter of 1940–1941. On the yellow cowling is the I/JG 3 Tatzelwurm in red. The pilot, *Feldwebel* Werner Bielefeldt, is from 7/JG 51. By the end of the Battle of Britain, Bielefeldt had shot down two aircraft.

This Bf 109E-4/B of Stab II/JG 54 was being flown by *Leutnant* Paul Steindl when it was photographed in late 1940/early 1941. After a period in Germany between 29 November 1940 and 27 January 1941, II/JG 54 returned to France until 29 March 1941. Steindl was a respected Austrian fighter pilot who also flew with JG 26, and had nine kills by the time of his death in an accident on 9 January 1945.

This Bf 109E-1 was in a hangar at Biggin Hill when this picture was taken in 1941. It appears to have had a section cut from its yellow cowling, a piece similar to the JG 53 *Pik As* badge. It is believed that this is Bf 109E-1/B Wk Nr 6730, Black 3+I of 8/JG 53, which was shot down near Goudhurst in Kent on 2 October 1940. The pilot, *Gefreiter* Heinz Zag, was captured. In addition to the yellow cowling, the rudder was yellow and the spinner red.